READ TO LEAD

By Ron Smith

Dwight –
May God Bless You
Ron 3/26/2004

Read to Lead
Copyright © 2004

Ron Smith
501 Blacktail Road
Lakeside, MT 59922
www.ronsmithbooks.com

All Scripture references taken from the Revised Standard
Version unless noted.
ISBN 0-9641913-5-0

Printed in the United States of America.

"In the best books, great men talk to us, give us their most precious thoughts, and pour out their souls into ours. God be thanked for books. They are the voices of the distant and the dead, and make us heirs of the spiritual life of past ages. Books are true levelers. They give to all, who will faithfully use them, the society, the spiritual presence, of the best and greatest of our race."

William Ellery Channing

READ TO LEAD

**In Honor of Laura Bush
First Lady of the United States
(2000-2004)**

An advocate for reading

Table of Contents

Why Write Read to Lead?

As a teenager, Legson Kayira walked 3,000 miles across Africa, beginning in 1958. Why? Legson desired an education, and his illiterate parents could not provide that for him. He finally met missionaries who pressed Skagit College in Washington to accept him. Kayira's desire to learn did not end there. He concluded his education at Cambridge University in England where he eventually became a professor of political science. He read the story of Booker T. Washington, the freed American slave, and was inspired to learn. Legson pushed across Africa to America and back to Cambridge.

Mark Twain wrote that people who can read but don't might as well be illiterate.

As an elementary schoolboy in New Mexico, my father tutored me week by week at my kitchen table. I learned, spelled and defined about fifty words per week. All of this started during my second or third grade, and these kitchen table lessons lasted through part of my junior high school years. I entered spelling bee after spelling bee; I never won but came close a few times.

Somewhere along the way, my father and mother convinced me of the importance of words on a page. Among other things, I document the reading power of parents in the following pages.

Lillian Carter's reading habits influenced young Jimmy. C.S. Lewis' biographer states that Lewis was well read by the age of eight. Susanna Wesley pushed her sons, John and Charles, to read. They both went to Oxford and later shook all of England with social reform and gospel preaching. Words strike with power on book pages.

Literacy decreases day by day in many parts of the world often replaced by television. Why do so many people

choose television over books? Is it laziness, or does it run
deeper? Mikhail Gorbachev stated it well in a C-Span
interview:

> Books should not be replaced by anything, by TV or
> by any such thing, because books make it possible to
> think more deeply. Probably American audiences,
> will say, 'Well, Gorbachev knows that we're reading
> less than we used to.' Well, I know that in all countries
> people are spending more time watching TV than
> reading. But still, I think that books will continue to
> exist. There will always be books. Television has a
> role of course. Television has a role in terms of
> allowing people to spend time at leisure. But in terms
> of formative work for the individual, it's very
> important to read books.

Robert Caro read 650,000 pages in the Lyndon
Baines Johnson Library. He accomplished this feat in order
to write Johnson's biography. Cultural change is necessary,
and we need a change in a big way. Five hours a day of
television do not produce Robert Caros.

Martin Gilbert, Winston Churchill's biographer,
worked full time, day after day, for thirty years. He read
Churchill's archives to properly reconstruct Churchill's life and
leadership for a reading public. Speaking of Churchill, Gilbert
says,

> Churchill read an enormous amount. He was
> almost the only person I've come across who, before
> he went to bed, would arrange for all the newspapers
> which were published in our country to arrive at about
> midnight. He didn't just read the London Times; he
> read the London Times, and the Guardian, and the
> News Chronicle, and the popular papers, and the mass
> circulation papers, and even the communist paper.
> He only cut out the communist paper when his wife

said, 'Darling we must cut down on the papers. We haven't got enough money.'

All cultural progress comes with a price tag. Readers pay a large part of that cultural price tag.

"We need to get back to the early fathers of our country," is an oft-heard refrain. We hold them up as role models. We think of people like President John Adams. His biographer, Joseph Ellis, writes, "John Adams read a lot. Even in his old age when his eyes were so bad, he had people read to him."

A college education in the United States costs a great deal. Some writers deem reading itself as an education. Richard Reeves, biographer for John F. Kennedy, states, "It was only in later life that I learned you could just sit and read books and that was an education." Benjamin Disraeli's biographer, Stanley Weintraub, says,

> What I remember most about my father was that he was a tremendous reader although he had very little education. I think he didn't have formal education beyond the fourth grade. But when he died in his sleep, he was found (to have been) reading Shakespeare's Othello.

Dr. James Billington, Librarian of Congress, wrote about his father's education:

> My father was a book collector. He collected used books from Leary's, and that was a wonderful introduction to scholarship. We had maybe two thousand or three thousand books.
>
> My father was an insurance broker. But he really was a teacher of people. He went into the insurance business and never got to complete his education, as he said in later years when they asked him for his biography, he always said—he went to

Leary's university, because it was this used bookstore. I guess that's why I'm a librarian of Congress, because my father kept bringing back used books from Leary's Bookstore in Philadelphia....

It was very interesting reading these used books growing up because they had underlining in them...It was a kind of education far better even than the very good education I later got at Princeton and Oxford.

The list goes on and on. Lenin's biographer, David Remnick, said on July 25, 1993, "My parents are readers. My father is a very serious reader." Stanley News wrote, "My dad was a bad guy. He was a criminal...My mother...was very big on reading and studying. When I was young, if I would be staying up late and listening to records, or reading books, or something—[and] my brother and sister would complain about it, she'd say, 'You know, he's the artistic type. Don't bother him.'"

The great British preacher Charles Spurgeon never went to college. He read six books a week for thirty-seven years of ministry. This challenges us. President Bill Clinton rattled fifteen authors off of the top of his head in an interview on C-Span. We need to be confronted by President Richard Nixon. He said, "I would urge all people who are in public life, who are trying to get into it, to spend less time in front of the tube—even if you're listening to this program [a TV show] and more time reading."

Harry Truman stated, "All readers can't be leaders, but all leaders must be readers."

"The task of the educated mind is simply put: read to lead."

Cicero (106-43 B.C.)

"No matter what his rank or position may be, the lover of books is the richest and the happiest of the children of men."

John Alfred Langford

"Amusement is the satisfaction of those who cannot think; entertainment is the gratification of those who cannot read."

Alexander Pope
(1688-1744)

"Naturally since I myself am a writer, I do not wish the ordinary reader to read no modern books. But if he must read only the new or only the old, I would advise him to read the old."

C.S.Lewis

C.S. Lewis
Literary Critic, Writer and
Radio Preacher

The Best Read Man of his Generation
-Literary Critic, William Empson

Biographical Sketch

Born:
> November 29, 1898
> Belfast, Ireland

Early Reading Influence:
> Two people, his mother, also a
> babysitter, Lizzie Endicott

Education:
> Oxford BA (Triple major graduated first in
> his class in all 3 majors: Classics, Philosophy,
> English)

Leadership:
> Literary Critic
> Educator (30 years at Oxford, 10 years at
> Cambridge)
> Social commentator
> Wrote twenty books, with ***Lion, Witch and
> the Wardrobe*** being the most famous

Died:
> November 22, 1963

Well-Read at Eight Years Old
A Life-Long Prodigious Reader

The world lost three historical giants on November 22, 1963: John F. Kennedy, Aldous Huxley (author of *Brave New World*), and last but not least, C.S. Lewis. The overwhelming shock of an assassinated, charismatic President of the United States overshadowed the deaths of the two others. C.S. Lewis will easily hold his own place easily in the broad sweep of history. Many 20th century Church historians consider Lewis to be the most influential Christian thinker of that century.

Lewis was born in 1898 to a solicitor (lawyer) and his wife (a preacher's daughter) in Belfast, Ireland. Clive Staples Lewis came from a long line of readers. George Sayer writes that Lewis' great great grandfather "gave to his children the advantage of being able to learn to read and write at the little church school in the village, and a faith to which the family for the next one hundred years remained unswervingly loyal" (p.22).

Oxford University admitted C.S. Lewis in 1916. In the middle of his education, he went to the front lines for two years during World War I and was wounded. Lewis graduated at the top of his class with three majors from the most prestigious English-speaking university in the world. He graduated first in Classics in 1920, ranking first in Philosophy in 1922, and first in English in 1923. Oxford kept him as a tutor for the next thirty years. Then, in 1954, he went to Cambridge as a full professor. He was there until his death in 1963.

Somewhat surprisingly, his mother, Flora "does not seem to have read to her children, taught them nursery rhymes, or told them bedtime stories" (p. 43). A babysitter and friend, Lizzie Endicott, read and told stories to young Lewis. She read to him, at the age two and a half, the usual kids fairy tales.

His mother began tutoring her son in academics around the age of eight. She gave him lessons every morning in French, Latin, and math and occasionally went on walks with him in the afternoon. More often, she rested and left him free to do whatever he wanted. He was very soon reading as voraciously as she and more widely.

The Lewis' house contained many books because both his parents bought and kept the books that they wanted to read. Jack, Lewis' nickname from an early age, had unrestricted access to their books. According to his biographer, Sayer, he was well read by the age of eight. He read all the books about animals:

[Including such] stories as **Black Beauty**. He read **Strand Magazine** from cover to cover, especially enjoying the magic stories of E. Nesbit: 'The Phoenix and the Carpet,' 'The Story of the Amulet,' and a little later on, 'The Magic City.' These formed his idea of what children's stories should be like.

A complete list of books that he had read by the age of nine would be very long. Some were advanced even by the standards of Macaulay's s choolboy. Some reveal lifelong tastes acquired at an early age. Take, for instance, his diary entry of March 5, 1908: 'I read **Paradise Lost**, reflections thereon.'

In the last days of his life, he was still reading *Paradise Lost* and reflecting thereon.

He had acquired the habit of writing by ten years old. He spent some time every day and most of his time on rainy days in the attic writing and illustrating books. At the age of ten years old, he produced a bibliography, a 'list of my books,' seven items, including a novel... (p. 51,Sayer).

Around age twelve, he began to seriously pray and read his Bible. At the same time, he read *Ben Hur* and *The Last Days of Pompeii* "for the scenes of cruelty, the beatings of slaves, and the gruesome performances of gladiators in the arena." In later life, Lewis condemned his own youthful lust for violence and sex. He also acquired his lifelong avid reading of science fiction at this time. He read H.G. Wells, *War of the Worlds* and similar works. Lewis bought massive quantities of books, which was a "life long habit." "He knew that if he really liked a book, he would want to read it again and would find a new delight in it when he did" (p. 103). About two thousand volumes of Lewis' book purchases live on at Wheaton College in Illinois.

At the age of sixteen, he began reading many of the classical English novels. He devoured Waverly, Jane Austen, Bronte, as well as some of the Victorian writers, Gaskell and Trollope. During this time he read many of the books that became favorites for life. The list is gargantuan but, nevertheless, worth mentioning. Some of his newly acquired favorites from this time listed by Sayer included:

> *The Crock of Gold, Phantasies, Faerie Queen, Arcadia,* the works of William Morris, Milton, Keats, Shelley, *Canterbury Tales*...By and large he formed his literary tastes in his teens and hardly altered them. Even then he had an astonishing gift for distinguishing the best from the second-rate... (p. 108, 109).

Lewis   wrote his own striking tales out of this wealth of personal reading.

It was for these various tales that Oxford kept Lewis from a full professorship. His fellow professors felt that stories such as *Out of the Silent Planet* or *The Hideous Strength* or *The Lion, The Witch and The Wardrobe* were simply below an Oxford Literary critic. They were not "scholarly enough" to merit a full professorship at historic Oxford. Children's stories were not the substance of an Oxford professor. Cambridge thought otherwise as well as the reading public. Lewis' popularity with the common man was much greater than simply a "reading public."

During World War II, Lewis carried on a weekly BBC radio broadcast as he brought Christian hope to the masses in England. His personal correspondence became so heavy that he had to hire several secretaries to help him answer his mail. Hiring the secretaries was difficult for Lewis because he took very seriously the problems of those who wrote to him. This is an accurate reflection of his overt concern for people. Further demonstrating his concern for people, Lewis spent many hours with a young mentally handicapped boy as he tried to teach the youngster how to read.

Lewis displayed his concern for students and his desire for their success in his classroom demeanor. He exercised great personal discipline in preparation for each Oxford tutorial session he oversaw and for each lecture he delivered. Lewis always read just before these lectures. He reviewed, with discipline, the material (usually already studied and often already memorized) for the scheduled class time.

George Sayer describes meeting Lewis after being directed to his office by Lewis' friend, J. R. Tolkien (author of the *Lord of the Rings*):

'Tell me Sayer, why do you want to read English?' he asked.

'I suppose it's mainly because I enjoy reading, especially poetry.'

'Well, that's a good answer. What poetry do you like?'

'Oh, lots. Wordsworth, Shelley, Keats, and, of course, Shakespeare.'

'Have you read any long poems, such as *The Prelude*?'

'No, I haven't read that,' I said. (In fact, I did not know who had written it.) 'But I've read some of the *Revolt of Islam* and the whole of *The Ballad of the White Horse.*'

'Good. What can you quote from that?'

I quoted the one verse that had stuck in my memory… 'The great Gaels of Ireland are the men that God made mad.' I got no further on my own, for which gusto and a glowing face he declaimed the next lines with me:

'For all their wars are merry, and all their songs are sad' (p. xx). Lewis continued and concluded the poem.

Any student who came to Lewis' class unprepared was better off dead. He had no time for lazy students or guile in his classes.

Lewis sometimes learned from his students in the class; this is a remarkable trait of humility in anyone's book. He showed true interest in what his students knew and endeavored to carry on true dialogue with them about it. Lewis recited long passages, often verbatim, from the literature under discussion and urged his students to do the same thing.

His disciplined preparation as a student at Oxford paralleled his later discipline as a professor. Before his English classes in 1922, as a student at Oxford, he spent two months reading "Seneca, Thucydides, Jonson, Croce,

Aristotle, Solona and the very early Attic writers, Freud, Havelock Ellis, Spenser, Kant, Strindberg, William James, Myers, Bradley, Hume, Gosse and Raleigh…" (p. 16).

A year earlier he studied: Homer, Virgil, Lucretius, Catullus, Tacitus, Herodotus, Cicero, Demosthenes. He read in French, works by Voltaire, Stendahl, Anatole Freance, Balzac, and many others. He also learned Italian, beginning with Dante's *Inferno.*

Lewis took a holiday, at the age of eighteen, at a place named Little Lea. While there, he read:Hawthorne, Aeschylus, Arnold Bennett, Edward Fitzgerald, Robert Bridges, Newman, Catullus, Herrick, Apollonius, Maeterlinck, Sir Thomas More, Tennyson, Mangan and several other writers (p. 116). One of Lewis' early tutors stated, "He has read more classics than any I ever heard of unless it be an Addison, or Landor, or Macaulay" (p. 114).

Lewis took pains to read everything necessary before a particular course began which he was responsible to oversee or teach. Non-athletic Lewis even studied football because one of his incoming students was the captain of the football team.

In 1944, he began working on *English Literature in the Sixteenth Century,* which was a part of the *Oxford History of English Literature (Volume 16).* Lewis' copious preparation for this task was mammoth. His biographer, Sayer (also an English Professor), writes, "He [Lewis] did an immense amount of reading for this project because he refused to give an opinion on a book he had not read." Lewis did not simply recite popular literary opinion on the era he was covering. Lewis shocked and stunned prevailing wisdom of the time with statements like, "the Renaissance never existed," "the humanists were inhumane, intolerant Philistines," and continud to buck the trend of literary criticism. Lewis said, "The new learning created the new ignorance" (p. 324). Lewis praised John Calvin, Tyndale, and Shakespeare.

The editors at Oxford University chose Lewis to write the critical volume on Shakespeare's century. This is probably because the editors knew that Lewis would literally read everything ever written in English during this century. This is confirmed by Sayer's statement that Lewis' volume "consists of a review of all the major and many minor writers of the period." Tolkien, *The Hobbit* king, reviewed Lewis' contribution to the *Oxford History of English Literature* and summed it up as "a great book." Lewis' volume outsells all other volumes of this history.

The life of the great Lewis ended in a nursing home, fittingly, with Bible reading around 5:00 p.m. daily (in any translation), a glass or two of dry sherry over a cigarette, and dinner at 7:30 p.m. Lewis concluded each day by choosing a book, usually to reread-very fast, as he was a firm believer in the necessity to read good books more than once.

Colin Duriez writes in the *C.S Lewis Encyclopedia*, according to the eminent literary critic William Empson, "Lewis was the best-read man of his generation, one who read everything and remembered everything he read."

November 22, 1963 for Lewis was the curtain call on a drama far greater than the impact of the ones he studied. The "best-read man of his generation" continues to speak today.

Dr. Ben Carson
History Making Neuro-Surgeon

*Two books a week in the fifth grade-
Assigned by his mother, with book reports*

Biographical Sketch

Born:
> September 18, 1951

Early Reading Influence:
> Mother

Education:
> BA Yale
> MD University of Michigan

Leadership:
> First neurosurgeon to separate Siamese
> twins joined congenitally at the head
> Led a team of eighty-seven doctors and nurses
> through the surgery

> Has written three books and received numerous
leadership awards.

"Read, Read, Read!"

*Ben Carson wishes all American role models
would say this to youth.*

Camera bulbs flashed as Dr. Benjamin Carson made history on September 6, 1987. After twenty-two hours of surgery, he and his team separated Siamese twins joined at the head. A team of seventy doctors, nurses, and technicians planned this monumental achievement for five months prior.

How did a black kid from the ghetto of Detroit ever get there? It was by reading and reading and reading some more.

Dr. Carson's father left his family, never to return, when young Ben was only eight years old. His mother, Sonya, although crushed and psychologically damaged, pressed on to raise young Ben and his older brother Curtis. Sonya was only in her twenties; she married at the age of thirteen and only completed a third grade education.

Not long after this shock, Sonya Carson began to press young Benjamin to memorize his multiplication tables. She also encouraged the boys in their intelligence and pushed them to the limit to achieve in school. Their grades went up, and Carson later stated that his "scores soared" (*Gifted Hands* p. 35*).* His school mates no longer called him "dummy."

Sonya pushed harder. Soon, she shut off the TV in the middle of a program, as the boys watched, and she declared a partial moratorium on the TV; young Ben and Curtis would read from then on. She instituted the life-changing program, which forced them to read and drastically curtail TV time.

From then on, he and his brother made regular visits to the local library. Their assignment was to read two books per week, and deliver a book report on each book to Sonya (their loving matriarchal taskmistress). Carson wrote that he chose books on animals, nature and science because of his love for those topics. His grades went up, his vocabulary automatically improved and by the seventh grade, Carson was at the top of his class. No doubt, his Christian faith further propelled him toward excellence as well.

At the age of thirteen, Ben received a subscription to *Psychology Today* magazine from his brother as a birthday present. He also read other psychology books to complement the magazine articles. At that time, he decided to become a psychiatrist—He did not change his mind until he went to medical school.

He scored in the 90th percentile on his S.A.T. and the Ivy League schools flocked to his Detroit home to woo him with scholarships. West Point offered him a full-scholarship. He later stated that most of the top colleges in the country had "contacted me with offers and inducements" (Ibid. p. 71).

Poverty gnawed at the Carson family, young Ben had only ten dollars to submit an application to one school. He applied to Yale, and the Connecticut school granted him a 90% scholarship.

Yale humbled young Ben. His classmates were just as smart as he was. The workload overwhelmed him and culminated in his freshman chemistry class. He wrote later in his autobiography that he "did not have the slightest hope of passing chemistry."

He prayed the night before a final exam, and God gave him a dream that night with the exact questions and answers for the next day's chemistry test. Carson scored

ninety-seven percent on the final. He concluded from this
high score that God, indeed, had called him to be a doctor.
He finished Yale and was accepted to medical school.

How did Carson excel in medical school? His
statement in **Think Big** is very interesting for readers:

> I cut many lectures so that I could stay in my
> room and not be disturbed. And I read constantly
> and insatiably…
>
> My reading began with the required material,
> then I added other books related to the same topic…
>
> Most days, I read from six in the morning
> until eleven at night, using all the texts and related
> materials I had available (p. 223, 224).

Video games, MTV, and skateboarding did not deliver
his degree in neurosurgery. Consistent effort multiplied year
after year, and belabored sacrifice slowly delivered this
achievement.

What was the norm for his third year of medical
school? It was more reading: "Everything available in print
on the subject of neurosurgery became an article I had to
read." At this point, Carson was quite philosophical. He had
developed a strategy for study in medical school by the third
year and it was purely reading from sun up til sundown.
Quoting William Ellery Channing, Carson writes,

> In the best books, great men talk to us, give us their
> most precious thoughts, and pour out their souls into
> ours. God be thanked for books. They are the voices
> of the distant and the dead, and make us heirs of the
> spiritual life of past ages. Books are true levelers.
> They give to all, who will faithfully use them, the
> society, the spiritual presence, of the best and greatest
> of our race (Ibid. p. 211).

Carson desires that authority figures and over-achievers in our culture would proclaim three words: "Read, Read, Read!" (p. 214). He labeled public libraries as "the treasure chest of the world."

Baltimore Mayor Ken Schmoke, a fellow African-American Yale alumnus, caught Carson's attention while they both attended Yale. Schmoke, a similarly voracious reader, pushed the Baltimore city council to adopt the slogan "Baltimore, the City that Reads" (Ibid. p. 215). Harvard and Oxford also post Schmoke as an alumnus. There is little doubt that Schmoke read his way into and through these fine schools (just as Carson did through medical school).

Litigator Harvey Wachsman (a friend of Carson's) reads voraciously. Wachsman's children also read two books per week with book reports handed in at the conclusion.

Wachsman's children parallel the "Ben Carson Club." The "Ben Carson Club" require literary feats for membership. Throughout the nation, middle school children form these clubs themselves, without teacher supervision.

Three requirements for Club members include:
1. Read two books a week
2. Submit a book report on each book weekly
3. Limit TV viewing

Club meetings include practical tips on reading, avoiding TV watching, and mutual encouragement. Carson writes that these 6th to 8th graders "know the value of educating themselves."

From the ghetto to the surgery theater, reading lifted Benjamin Carson.

"Most Ignorance is vincible ignorance; we don't know because we don't want to know; we remain uninformed because we refuse to read."

Aldous Huxley
(1894-1963)

Ralph Nader
A Lawyer at $5,000
a Year

Seat Belts for the Cars
Labels on Cigarette Packages

Biographical Sketch

Born:
February 27, 1934
Winsted, Connecticut

Early Reading Influence:
Family
Early self-motivation

Education:
B.A. Princeton, Russian and Chinese
J.D.-Harvard Law School

Leadership:
Consumer Advocacy forcing corporate
responsibility, Nader and his associates have
published many books aiming to protect the
American Public

My Paradise

*Ralph Nader's label for the library
at Princeton University*

I recently told one of my students that I was writing about Ralph Nader's gargantuan reading habits. My student responded, "Who is Ralph Nader?" I talked about seat belts, no smoking on planes, and safety labels on cigarette packages. She responded, "Oh."

Nader was born on February 27, 1934, in Winsted, Connecticut. His primary school teachers wondered whether this young, Arabic-speaking, immigrant's kid could understand enough English to get by in the first grade. It is humorous to the point of ridiculous when we contrast the elementary teachers' attitudes about Ralph with Ralph's first memory of listening to complex English.

He describes going into the courthouse at the age of four, and listening to lawyers argue cases. He went home and told his mother that he had spent the day at the courthouse sitting on the floor to listen to the attorneys. As well, Nader argued with another friend at the age of nine over the merits and faults of Franklin D. Roosevelt's New Deal.

Charles McCarry tells us that during Nader's sophomore year in high school (at age 14), he brought home a large stack of the *Congressional Record*. The principal said nobody ever read them. Thus, young Ralph got them as a gift and read them. McCarry writes that to Nader, information is truth (*Citizen Nader*, p. 40). Nader graduated from high school in 1951 and went on to Princeton to study Chinese and Russian.

Princeton placed him, immediately, in a remedial English class. Nader loved Princeton. As well, he read in a manner that McCarry calls "voracious." Princeton produced a large amount of mythology around Ralph's reading and literary appetite. In fact, Ralph became a standing joke to some of his contemporaries because he was always in the library. Nader later stated that Princeton was his paradise (p. 43). People walked by him in the library hissing at him and making ribald remarks. One Princeton friend, Ted Jacobs, recalled the night that Nader took a book about Brazil to the toilet with him. Nader read the whole thing before he came back and was ready to discuss it with his friends.

According to McCarry, he read "forgotten books of social history, old copies of intellectual magazines, and studies of industrial relations." He graduated from Princeton with a low "A" average. One of his teachers stated, "He is the best undergraduate I have known in five years." From Princeton, Nader went on to Harvard Law School where he rebelled against the staid culture.

McCarry writes, "He flirted with the patience of the administration, cutting classes, disappearing for days at a time, devoting himself to outside interests." At times, he vanished for days and returned with a suntan. He traveled all the way to Mexico during school days to get it. Eventually, Nader graduated from Harvard without any remarkable academic achievements, other than the fact that he edited the school newspaper. One of his friends stated, "Ralph paid little attention to the curriculum. He got through because he was smart." This shows that Nader enjoyed life and was a bit unconventional.

Nader's career as the citizen's consumer advocate began when he wrote a blistering book in 1962 about the Chevrolet Corvair. It was entitled **Unsafe at Any Speed.** That book catapulted him into national fame, and he became one of the most respected men in the nation because he fought for the little guy. Nader took on and brought General Motors to its knees by applying what he learned in law school.

Psychologists would call Nader a workaholic. He works twenty-hour days. He speed-reads through many documents daily. Nader responds philosophically to these outcries of wonder and angst: "Americans understand the challenge in athletics, on the battlefield, and in economic competition. You wouldn't ask an Olympic swimmer or chess player why he works twenty hours a day." Nader appointed himself to a one-man mission for corporate responsibility around the world. In his mind, carrying out those missions requires Olympic-like devotion.

What does Ralph Nader's workplace look like? Robert Buckhorn describes it:

Nader's room behind a padlocked door marked with a painted number 1, was no more impressive or organized than any of the others. If anything, it gave the appearance of a niche allocated to an assistant professor at a not-too-well financed college. Books were piled on the floor, which was covered by a seedy rug. There were floor-to-ceiling bookshelves jammed with tomes ranging from the U.S. (legal) Code to Congressional directories, and Senate and House hearings. The desk was littered...with half finished work. Behind the desk, pinned to a drape, was a framed picture of Thomas Jefferson, the only picture in the room (p. 75-76).

Nader began taking on law students as summer interns in 1968, to teach them the ways of enforcing corporate responsibility. They were eventually termed "Nader's Raiders." What were they like?

"One of the raiders described the summer work load as the equivalent of doing a Ph.D. dissertation in ten weeks" (Buckhorn, p. 89). The Ph.D. analogy is a good one. Nader is in some ways a teacher at heart. Anyone who lectures Congress as much as Nader must be a teacher.

Another intern said,

When you are sitting there at two o'clock in the morning, going over thousands of documents page by page by page, thousands and thousands of pages, compiling things, gathering evidence, talking to people, you don't feel like a raider at all.... We play by the rules every step of the way...if you don't play by the rules, your credibility is going to be destroyed by personal attack....Believe me, when the investigation begins to hit pay dirt, they are going to be trying to find ways to discredit you, and there is no point in making it easy for them (Buckhorn, p. 83,84).

Between 1969 and 1971, the list of the Raiders' book-publishing accomplishments boggles the mind:

The Nader Report on the Federal Trade Commission

The Interstate Commerce Omission

Vanishing Air (air pollution)

The Chemical Feast (food and drug industries)

One Life-One Physician (self regulation of medicine)

Old Age: The Last Segregation

Water Lords (study of the Savannah River)

Water Wasteland (study of water pollution)

The Closed Enterprise System (study of anti-trust enforcement)

Citibank (a study of the inner workings)

Caution, This Job May Kill You
(occupational safety and health)
Report on Coal Mine Health and Safety in West Virginia
Sowing the Wind: Pesticides, Meat and Public Interest
Tractor Safety Report
Crash Safety in General Aviation Aircraft
The Company State
(study on duPont in Delaware)
Power and Land in California
Damming the West
On the Job...

Between 1966 and 1970, Nader accomplished "almost single-handedly" the following legislation for the American public:

Traffic and Motor Vehicle Safety Act
Natural Gas Pipeline Safety Act
Wholesale Meat Act
Radiation Control Act
Wholesale Poultry Products Act
Coal Mine Health and Safety Act
Occupational Health and Safety Act

As well, Nader fought for and helped bring about cigarette safety legislation. He is primarily responsible for the seat belt laws, as well as consumer-oriented class-action lawsuits. He reads volumes and makes his "Raiders" pore through thousands of documents—page by page by page. All of this to move America in the right direction.

During the late 1960s and early 1970s, Nader received more than ninety thousand pieces of mail per year. He has an unpublished address and an unlisted phone number. People address these letters in telling ways:

Ralph Nader, Washington, D.C.
Ralph Nader, The White House

Ralph Nader, A Well Known Washington Lawyer
Senator Ralph Nader
Ralph Nader, The Little Man's Representative
Ralph Nader, Everyman's Lawyer
Ralph Nader, Consumer Champion
Ralph Nader, The Greatest
One letter simply had his picture taped to it.

How does Nader respond to his mail? Buckhorn writes,

Nader spends long hours scanning the mail, and insists his staff do likewise. Any of them who don't hear *vox populi* in the letters or show less than the right amount of reverence or sympathy for the letter writers get a quick lecture on arrogance, delivered with snarls from Nader. One staff member termed the mail 'Nader's umbilical cord to the consumer.'

Nader also gets about one out of a thousand pieces of hate mail like the following:

Dear Mr. Nader,

You stupid son of a bitch. Why don't you try to educate the stupid drivers. Machines don't kill people, it's the dumb sons of bitches behind them. You should have learned this before now. But maybe you are as stupid as they are. Signed

A Driver of 61 years

His biographers point out that he does not answer all of his mail. He simply does not have the staff to do so. However, Buckhorn writes, "Nader is faithful in his letter reading. 'You can find him on a Sunday afternoon, or on a holiday reading letters. It's like he gets some kind of strength from them'" (p. 255). Nader feels deeply and philosophically about his mail which produces vitriolic responses toward his staff if it is handled arrogantly. He feels what the people feel and hears their cries through the mail. Nader says,

> It's very important to constantly keep your eye on the overall general objectives without forgetting that you're dealing with very concrete problems affecting people. And if they're affecting people, they're going to be what many of us may consider mundane, or trivial, or superficial, or wasteful, but they have to be developed. They have to be given consideration because they're real; because people are concerned about them. And anything that's going to endure is going to have relatively deep roots among the average citizens, otherwise it is going to be toppled very easily. It is very important to keep asking the question; what really bugs the average citizen? (p. 257, 258).

Nader listens to the average American; he reads their mail religiously. For this, the little man loves him. He has earned enormous respect from the "powers that be" in Washington D.C. because he masters facts with an unusual ability and presents them in a cogent way. Between 1966 and 1972, Nader appeared before thirty-nine different Senate and House subcommittees. He testified because of his precision and knowledge-based expertise in a broad range of multifaceted categories.

This young man drew laughter and jeers from his Princeton colleagues because of his omnivorous reading appetite. He brought General Motors to its knees over the Corvair. He continues to be the citizen's watchdog for corporate responsibility. He reads and adds to his enormous mental capacity a gargantuan work load. His genuine concern for people propels him further.

Nader writes, "I've got to set a very high standard. If I ever have to ask someone to work on New Year's Eve, I

48

want them to be sure that I have already done 17 times more work on the project than I am asking them to do"—Ralph Nader (Buckhorn, p. 296).

In some ways, Nader justifies the maverick in all of us.

*"Give me twenty-six lead soldiers
and I will conquer the world."*

Benjamin Franklin

Jimmy Carter
39th President of the
United States
1976-1980

A Hunger to Learn,
Tolstoy at Twelve,
Three Books a Week

Biographical Sketch

Born:
>October 24, 1924
>Plains, Georgia

Early Reading Influence:
>Mother

Education:
>U.S. Naval Academy B.S.

Leadership:
>Governor of Georgia 1970-74
>President of the U.S. 1976-80
>Received the Nobel Peace Prize 2002

>Jimmy Carter has also written several books

Jimmy Carter Reads at Meals— Like His Mother

Jimmy Carter's story starts with his grandfather, James Jackson Gordy. Jimmy's grandfather read a lot about politics. He owned a large personal library, which he used often. Around the turn of the 20th century, the Gordy's had a daughter named Lillian (who later became Jimmy's mother).

From her earliest days, Lillian combed her father's library. She read constantly from the time she was a little girl. In fact, James Wooten, one of Carter's biographers, states, "She spent whole days reading." Lillian spent the years of the Great Depression working ten and twelve hour days as a nurse. She worked at the hospital in Plains, Georgia, and in other places as well. At the age of sixty-seven, she went to India to work with the Peace Corps.

Lillian raised several children, all of whom loved books; this was partly due to her influence. Jimmy Carter, born October 1, 1924, was no exception.

President Carter said, "I'm more like my mother than I am my father...she is a reader. She reads day and night. At the breakfast table, lunch table, supper table. I did too. She encouraged it. And I still do" (Slosser, p. 21). The only exception was Sunday meals, they were too formal for reading.

Carter also credits much reading influence to an early schoolteacher, Miss Julia Coleman. He mentioned her, by name, in his presidential inaugural speech. Miss Coleman loved her students but was strict and demanded a lot from them. She found in Carter (according to his own words) a "hunger to learn." She cultivated that hunger and made it grow.

President James Earl Carter writes in his autobiography that whenever anyone asked what he wanted for Christmas or his birthday, his response was "books." He received the complete set of works by Guy de Maupassant when he was only four years old. Of course, he read these many years later.

He was heavily influenced by Miss Julia Coleman, who was the school superintendent. The students in the classrooms were required to debate, memorize, and recite long poems as well as Bible passages. They each had to learn a musical instrument as well as the basics of music.

When I was about twelve years old she called me in and stated that she was ready for me to read **War and Peace**. I was happy with the title because I thought finally Miss Julia had chosen for me a book about cowboys and Indians. I was appalled when I checked the book out of the library because it was about 1,400 pages long, written by the Russian novelist Tolstoy, and of course not about cowboys at all. It turned out to be one of my favorite books, and I have read it two or three times since then. The book is about the French army under Napoleon, who believed that he was destined to be the conqueror of the world....

As stated by Tolstoy the purpose of the book is to show the course of human events—even the greatest historical events—is determined ultimately not by the leaders but by the common ordinary people.... (***Why Not the Best?***)

Dr. James Billington, Librarian of Congress and overseer of twenty-five million books in the Library of Congress, read *War and Peace* at a young age also. Billington said that after *War and Peace* all other books seemed short.

Carter's mother recalls that Jimmy began reading international news during the summer of his ninth grade.

Miss Julia gave a silver star for every five books that her students read: she gave a gold one for every ten. James Wooten writes, "He kept count of how many [gold stars] he had whenever he got another one." Lillian recalled, "He'd come home and tell us about it." For several years, Miss Julia gave Jimmy long reading lists, and he dutifully completed them, star by golden star. Miss Julia's lists consisted of "histories, biographies, fiction light and heavy." Miss Coleman helped build Carter's enormous and exceedingly broad reading appetite.

Jimmy Carter graduated number one in his high school class, and Georgia Southwestern College granted him a full scholarship. He gave it to Eloise Ratliff, the number two ranking student, because her family could not afford to send her to college. So she accepted Jimmy's scholarship and went to Georgia Southwestern. Carter also attended Georgia Southwestern for one year, and then went on to Georgia Tech. After his year at Georgia Tech., he went to Annapolis, in the early 1940s, to the Naval Academy.

Speaking of the Naval Academy, Carter had been concerned in his high school years that the Plains High School did not have a full science curriculum which could prepare him for Annapolis. So he "with characteristic discipline...scoured the library and his teacher's shelves for any and all books he could find on chemistry and engineering and advanced mathematics." Jimmy's cousin, Hugh, states, "I don't recall seeing Jimmy without a book or several books in his hands or somewhere close by all during his high school days" (Wooten).

Carter looked back on his Navy days and said, "That was an opportunity for me that paid off…I had a chance to travel extensively. I read and studied, everything: music, art, drama and so forth. I stretched my mind, and had a great challenge, and I never had any regret for a single day that I spent in the Navy."

Carter told Admiral Hyman Rickover that he had not put forth all of his effort throughout his years in the Naval academy. The Admiral asked him the icy question, "Why not?" Carter stated, repeatedly, that Rickover's question was a defining moment in his life.

He took up the peanut business after he left the Navy and then became Governor of Georgia. How did he become known as a "walking encyclopedia" about peanuts? Wooten tells us,

> The Sumter county agricultural agents were of great assistance and the books they gave him were a fertile resource.…
>
> It was an exhausting grind. His days often spanned sixteen and eithteen hours…come home…collapse in the chair for a few moments…eat…then read himself to sleep on the latest farming techniques and innovations (p. 132).

As Governor of Georgia, Carter said,
Our people are our most precious possession, and we cannot afford to waste the talents and abilities given by God to one single Georgian. Every adult illiterate …is an indictment of us all. If Switzerland and Israel and other people can eliminate illiteracy so can we (Ibid. p. 300).

Carter attracted bookworms to his candidacy for President of the United States. Jody Powell, Carter's White House Chief of Staff, "read almost everything he could get his hands on…" (p. 283). Powell's mother reported this to Wooten about her son and his work for Carter. Powell foreshadowed another omnivorous reader in the White House, Ronald Wilson Reagan.

During the Presidential campaign, Robert Slosser wrote,

> Carter is well-read, and his interests range far afield from politics. Up to the start of the campaign his favorite authors were said to be William Faulkner, James Agee, and Dylan Thomas. Lately, said members of his family, he has concentrated on politics, philosophy, history, taxation policy and foreign affairs (p. 113).

Carter writes about his reading during the Presidential campaign of 1975-1976: "I've never failed, since we began the campaign in January to read a full chapter in the Bible every night in Spanish" (*Carpenter's Apprentice*, p. 46).

> I have always read three or four books each week, and it was easy and natural to revise my reading lists to encompass subjects relating more toward foreign affairs, defense, and economics. I accumulated and read histories and biographies concerning our nation and Presidency.

This is phenomenal. Tom Clancy stated on a C-Span interview that Ronald Reagan read the same amount during his later presidency. Incidentally, Reagan read *The Hunt for Red October* and launched Clancy's career.

A friend raised a good question with me about this: Is reading this much a realistic objective for each and every person, or is this an exceptional example? Carter and Reagan are leaders, made in part by their reading. They exemplify reading leaders. By contrast, non-reading leaders don't produce serious intellectual examples to follow.

How phenomenal is three or four books a week? Consider this: In 1986, Devine, Dissel, and Parrish published the *Harvard Guide to Influential Books (113 Eminent Harvard Professors Discuss the Books that Have Shaped Their Thinking)*. The editors found it necessary to point out that the head librarian for The Harvard Business School, Mary V. Chatfield, reads one book a week. The editors stated this biographical fact about no other professor at Harvard in 1986.

Carter stuns his readers with the statement, "in order to avoid mistakes, [I] even studied the campaign platforms of all the unsuccessful candidates for President since our electoral process began" (p. 162). Carter studied (loser-by-loser) all of the unsuccessful Presidential bids in the history of the United States. Imagine that! Carter himself (not his aides) studied over thirty failed candidacies. He read these chronicles of defeats while campaigning for the Presidency. He continues about his campaign reading:

> I read scientific journals about every conceivable source of energy, so I might understand the potential for meeting the world's need during the decades ahead. Nuclear disarmament proposals and agreements were studied, along with budgets of the different services within the defense department. A special effort was made to meet the authors of these books and articles, so I might obtain more information about their subjects at first hand. Later several of them provided me with prepublication drafts of their writings… (p. 162).

Things did not change after he became President. One writer stated that Carter literally read himself into the White House.

Victor Lasky writes in *Jimmy Carter, The Man and The Myth*,

We were told, for example, that the Chief Executive was considering policy and signing bills to the strains of Puccini, Wagner, Rachmaninoff and Amy Carter's violin. Moreover, he was reading passages from a Spanish language Bible every night (p. 14).

This passage underlines the colossal reading bent of this President.

Dr. Helmut Schmidt sent him an edition of the German national policy on energy, specially translated from German for Carter. Carter writes that he actually had to wait for the book. He thought that possibly Dr. Schmidt had forgotten it. (He had become Chancellor Schmidt since their discussion.) Carter had not forgotten it.

To Jimmy Carter, books satisfied a self-admitted "hunger to learn." This continual life-long literary feeding frenzy (three or four books a week) landed him in the White House in 1976.

Carter's family history thrust reading upon him. Others without that history have hope also. Legson Kayira is a prime example.

"In a very real sense, people who have read good literature have lived more than people who cannot, or will not read….It is not true that we can have only one life to live; if we can read, we can live as many more lives and as many kinds of lives as we wish"

S.I Hayakawa

Harry Truman
33rd President of the
United States
1945-1952

*Read Every Book in His Hometown
Library (3,000 Books Including the
Encyclopedias) by the Time He Graduated
From High School*

Biographical Sketch

Born:
> May 8, 1884
> Independence, Missouri

Early Reading Influence:
> Mother

Education:
> High School (Independence, Missouri)

Leadership:
> President of the U.S. 1945-52
> Vice-President 1944, 45
> U.S. Senator 1934-44
> Also wrote two volumes of memoirs 1955-1956

Died:
> December 26, 1972

A prayer of Harry Truman written on White House Stationary, August 15, 1950.

Oh! Almighty and Everlasting God, Creator of Heaven, Earth and the Universe: Help me to be, to think, to act what is right, because it is right; make me truthful, honest and honorable in all things; make me intellectually honest for the sake of right and honor and without thought of reward to me. Give me the ability to be charitable, forgiving, and patient with my fellow men—help me to understand their motives and their shortcomings—even as thou understandest mine!

Amen, Amen, Amen

Always Reading

Harry Truman explains this prayer in his own handwriting:

The prayer on this page has been said by me—by Harry S. Truman—from high school days, as window washer, bottle duster, floor scrubber in an Independence, Missouri, drugstore, as a timekeeper on a railroad contract gang, as an employee of a newspaper, as a bank clerk, as a farmer riding a gang plow behind four horses and mules, as a fraternity official learning to say nothing at all if good could not be said of a man, as a public official judging the weaknesses and shortcomings of constituents, and as President of the United States of America (Hilman, introduction for *Mr. President*).

Harry Truman's story begins with his mother and includes school teachers, much like Jimmy Carter's. About Truman's mother, one of his biographers writes,

Martha Ellen Young was a slender tiny girl with dark hair parted in the middle and eyes alive with laughter and mischief. An outdoor girl who rode a horse as if she were born on a sidesaddle, she was also a voracious reader who, in later years, adopted the appalling past time of reading the Congressional Record from cover to cover each day that Congress was in session. At the Baptist College for Women in

Lexington, she revealed strong talent in music and art and an ability to flaunt Baptist decree with impunity by attending dances (Steinberg, p. 19).

She read "voraciously" all her life. Even after Truman went into political office, at times, she called Truman and told him how to vote on issues.

Physicians diagnosed Truman as having "flat eyeballs" when he was six years old. He began wearing glasses (that looked like the bottom of Coke bottles) which magnified the size of his blue eyes. This also kept him from the usual rough and tumble boyhood military games and athletic endeavors. Later in life, Truman termed himself as a "sissy" growing up. Truman's biographer, Ralph Martin, writes that because of his poor eyesight and huge expensive glasses, "he turned to books" (Martin, p. 10).

Three other factors encouraged this "turning to books." His parents, the availability of a decent town library, and two caring teachers through his youth pushed Truman to reading greatness. Truman had family support, an accessibility to books, and some kind of follow-up from his early teachers to see how he fared.

Truman was later asked in an interview during his Presidency, "I understand that you feel you learned a good deal about politics from Plutarch's Lives and that your father read it aloud to you when you were a boy." To which the President responded,

He did. We saved our dimes, threw them into the tray of an old trunk, and they accumulated faster than you'd think even in those days, and then my father sent away, or maybe it was my mother, but one of them sent away, and we got the nicest set of Shakespeare you ever did see and a book of Plutarch's Lives. It had a bright red cover, and you're right. My father used to read me out loud from that.

And I've read Plutarch through many times since. I never have figured out how he knew so much. I tell you, they just don't come any better than old Plutarch. He knew more about politics than all the other writers I've read put together (Miller p. 69).

Truman stated, later in life, that he read the Bible through completely two times by the age of twelve, having begun the first Bible venture at age six. He recalled never being bored as a result of all of the reading, and that he loved all of his elementary school teachers.

In fact, Truman achieved so well in elementary school that he skipped the third grade (a fact which he later made light of in a White House interview). Skipping a grade indicated nothing of Truman's early learning. That crux of his early learning was his shark-like appetite for books. This appetite continued throughout his life.

Outstanding biographer, David McCullough wrote in 1992,

By now (the fourth grade) he also was reading 'everything I could get my hands on-histories and encyclopedias and everything else.' For his tenth birthday, his mother presented him with a set of large illustrated volumes in 1884 grandly titled in gold leaf *Great Men and Famous Women*. He would later count that moment as one of his life's turning points.

There were four volumes: *Soldiers and Sailors, Statesmen and Sages, Workmen and Heroes*, and *Artists and Authors*. They were anthologies of essays from Harper's and other leading American and English magazines, not books for children...he would one day confide to a friend that he studied the careers of 'great men.'

Truman and his best friend, Charlie Ross, decided on a youthful long-term literary project together. Charlie was the son of the town jailor of Independence, Missouri. (Charlie became the White House Press Secretary for Truman during Truman's Presidency.) The two boys decided around the age of twelve to read all the books in the entire library of Independence, Missouri, by the time they graduated from high school. Later students estimated the numbers to be anywhere from two thousand volumes to six thousand volumes. Truman stated that there were three thousand. Both Charlie Ross and Harry Truman read all of those volumes by the end of their teen years–including the encyclopedias. Truman later stated that he always had is head in a book, and they were mostly history books (Miller, p. 25). This led to life-long learning and self-education for Truman and his friend Charlie.

Truman's mother played a very formative role, along with two school teachers, in his appetite to learn—just like Jimmy Carter. Three teachers, Matilda Brown, Margaret Phelps, and Ardelia Palmer, formed Truman. Truman's love for Latin persisted through his whole life. Mrs. Palmer stated that his friend and Press Secretary, Charlie Ross, was "quicker than he" but what Truman learned "it seemed he never did forget." Many of Truman's biographers have made the same point. Truman's learning style resembled that of a slow tape recorder—never fast to learn, but he never forgot things he learned.

It is interesting that there are so many examples of women encouraging these young men to read. Is this cultural, or was it indicative of the time? Was reading seen as a "woman's hobby" while men worked to support their families?

Truman read his Bible in his adolescent years and his Bible was important to him. His mother stated, "When we all got into an argument, they always said Harry was best posted in the Bible because he read all the history and the stories in it" (Steinberg, p. 25).

As a young man, Truman worked in a clothing store directly after his marriage to Bess. One of his co-workers, Bluma Jacobson, stated,

> There were slack days as well as good days, and if Harry wasn't around, you could always look up in t he balcony, and Harry would be up there with a book, reading or studying. He studied law a good deal in those days. Just picking it up, he did not go to law school at the time. He went to night school in Kansas City later, and studied law, but at the time you would always find him reading a book (Miller, p. 110).

Judge Albert Ridge stated that Harry, during his younger adult years, "was always reading two or three books at a time and always making notes in the margins, especially in history books. Frequently…very often he knew much more than the writer, the historian, and he would use…his favorite word was "bunk," and I guess it still is" (p.11).

Truman went to the Kansas City Law School for two years where he attained a "B" average. He eventually dropped out. He cited outside interests as the reasons for his quitting. Although he dropped out of law school, he never stopped reading. His daughter, Margaret, stated that she could never remember seeing her father without a book in his hand (McCullough, p. 191).

When Truman was elected to the Senate in 1935, "he talked about books, his continuing interest in Latin, and said that he did not expect to be very busy as a freshman Senator. In his spare time, he told them, he planned to enroll at Georgetown University's night law school" (Steinberg, p. 124). He spoke of just aging away somewhere during his time in the Senate and reading Plutarch and Shakespeare "over and over and over" (McCullough, p. 281). His daughter remembered that during his time in the Senate, he got a lot of reading in apart from his usual senatorial duties. Truman read political, historical, business, military, and biographical themes.

Truman took the Presidency after the death of Franklin D. Roosevelt in the mid 1940s. Truman also took his voracious reading into the White House. Presidential biographer Hillman, writes,

> President Truman probably knows as much about the history of the Presidency as any man who ever sat in the White House. He has been a close student of the conduct and ideas of every President, even to the extent of knowing what practically every cabinet officer since Washington's time did to help or hinder the functioning of the Presidency. There is hardly a problem confronting him today for which he cannot quickly cite a parallel in the past (Hillman, p. 86, 87).

This vast knowledge reminds one of Carter. As well, Truman felt that Jefferson and Jackson had the most impact on his work. When asked to give an overview of which Presidents influenced him the most, Truman chronicled the strengths and weaknesses of Jefferson, Jackson, Lincoln, Hayes, Cleveland, Wilson, and Roosevelt (Hillman, p. 88).

Similar to Carter, Harry S. Truman studied the history of unsuccessful Presidential campaigns. He pored through the history of special press criticisms of all preceding Presidents with the same motive as Carter. He did not want to repeat the mistakes of the past.

Historians describe Truman as a giant in military history. He stated one time that the thing which distinguished great generals from all the rest was bravery and a willingness to go to the front lines with their men. Truman saw Hannibal as the greatest of all military figures in history, second was Alexander, third was Napoleon. Truman held Robert E. Lee as the greatest American general followed closely by Omar Bradley. Truman disdained Douglas McArthur. He directed his wrath, as well, toward General (later to be President) Dwight Eisenhower. Truman called McArthur "God" sarcastically and labeled Eisenhower "illiterate."

Truman continued reading the Bible in the White House where he staunchly defended the King James Version. He always turned to Plutarch for political advice. General Bradley stated, "President Truman was always reading things." Truman's Secretary of State, Dean Acheson, quipped, "Mr. Truman read, I sometimes think, more than any of the rest of us." The Chief Justice of the Supreme Court, Vinson, discussed a bill in Congress with Truman. Vinson quoted the Latin writer, Cato, in Latin and Truman corrected him in saying, "That's the idea, but you didn't say it right." Later scholars pointed out that Truman was right and Vinson was wrong when quoting Cato.

In spite of all his respect for his earlier school teachers, Truman respected neither formal education nor formal textbooks. Later in life, during an interview, Truman was asked about his reading and answered,

> The thing I found out from reading was that there is damn little information in most schoolbooks that was worth a damn. If you wanted to find out why France was against England during the Revolution and why and wherefore of Jefferson's being able to buy Louisiana, you had to go and look it up for yourself. It didn't matter how good your teachers were. They never taught you things like that (Miller, p. 64).

This man who never went to college was a President who "was a prodigious reader, and each night he would carry home a portfolio, often six or eight inches thick, the next morning he would have gone through all that material and taken such action as was needed" (McCullough, p. 557).

A reporter asked him during a Presidential interview:

> 'Mr. President, can you remember a time

when you haven't read?'

'No, I can't, not unless I was sick, and even then if I could manage it, I'd prop up a book and read on the sickbed- glasses or not, I was always reading. I've never regretted it either, and I suppose considering the fact that I became President of the United States, it wasn't time wasted' (Miller, p. 53).

Truman is a fine demonstration of the rewards of hard work in reading, as well as someone who would not follow the "normal" path. His life also shows that the information is out there, but often one must go out and find it.

This self-educated, non-college graduate once stated, "Every reader can not be a leader, but every leader must be a reader."

"When I get a little money, I buy books; and if there is any left, I buy food and clothes."

Desiderius Erasmus
(1466-1536)

Charles Spurgeon
Britain's Most Eloquent
Preacher

Six Books a Week for Thirty-Seven Years
He Read Everything

Biographical Sketch

Born:

June 19, 1834
Kelvedon, Essex, England

Early Reading Influence:

Self motivated

Education:

No college degree, some primary and secondary-school education

Leadership:

Preaching (Largest church in the world in the 1800's)
Started a training College that continues today
Wrote more than 50 books.

Died:

January 1892, and 100,000 people lined streets of London for his funeral

A Great Weight of Learning

Charles Spurgeon was born one of seventeen children on June 19, 1834. He never went to college but published more than any other author in Church history with more than sixty-seven large volumes to his credit. Reading his work would take a virtual lifetime, much less writing the way he did. His book, *All of Grace,* sold well over a million copies—one of three which ultimately sold over a million copies. He preached to over one million people, face to face. Eric Hayden writes,

> Spurgeon missed being admitted to college because a servant girl inadvertently showed him into a different room than that of the principal who was waiting to interview him. Later, he determined not to reapply for admission when he believed God spoke to him, 'Seekest thou great things for thyself? Seek them not!' (Twenty-first century reader, take note).

His lack of formal education did not keep him from personal self-education. He read Bunyon's work *Pilgrim's Progress* for the first time at the age of six and went on to read it over one hundred times through his lifetime. Spurgeon read and read fast.

Spurgeon read whole paragraphs like most of us read sentences. Church historian Mark Hopkins writes,

> The reason for Spurgeon's stability was that he found in the Puritans' theology ample material to help him fashion his own although his own Bible study was

this influence, his theological emphases were different from those of most evangelicals of the period.

One writer stated that Spurgeon knew more Puritan theology as a teenager than the Puritans themselves.
Vast knowledge requires a vast storehouse. Spurgeon's library numbered more than twelve thousand volumes. The evangelist could walk into his library on command and find a passage from a book that he had read years before. This led, as well, to informed preaching. Dr. Lewis Drummond writes,

> Spurgeon had an eloquence that gives the impression he labored hours over his similes, metaphors, and dramatic illustrations. Yet he prepared his Sunday morning sermon Saturday night, and his Sunday night sermon on Sunday afternoon. He would walk into the pulpit with a simple, small outline, sometimes written on the back of an envelope, and from that extemporaneously pour forth eloquence almost equal to Shakespeare's.

Spurgeon read a book a day, and this helped his performance in the pulpit. No one preaches with that "Saturday night-Sunday afternoon" kind of preparation unless one reads voraciously. One scholar of the day stated,

> [Spurgeon was] a great weight of learning, but he never paraded it. He was an omnivorous reader, had something like Macaulay's faculty for swift reading, and had an eye so rapid and a mind so acute he could take in paragraphs as most readers take in sentences, and he could remember what he read." Another professor said, "He knew so much that it was unnecessary for him to make a parade of knowledge...

Spurgeon established a Bible college because of his respect for learning and wellspring of knowledge. This college continues today and still trains preachers. One biographer writes,

> In the college the great event of the week was the Friday afternoon lecture. There would be readings from the poets on occasion. Young's Night Thoughts was a favorite as were Milton, Cowper, Wordsworth and Coleridge, and Dr. Hamilton's 'Christian classics.' Mr. Spurgeon often quoted from the Puritan writers. Always the reading or the lecture was in itself a lesson in elocution.

Because of his lack of formal education one church publication in England was forced to write,

> A greater mistake cannot be made than that which thinks or speaks of Mr. Spurgeon as an uneducated man. He was the master of an English style, which many a scholar might envy, and which was admirably fitted, for his purposes. This style could only have been acquired by great pains and by the constant study of the best literary models, which it recalls. Mr. Spurgeon's knowledge of the Bible was, of course, thorough.

One author writes,

> He cared little for authority, or the formulas of creeds and articles, and instead of confining himself to the language of the schools, and of previous divines and theologians, he would ransack the stores of modern literature, profane as well as sacred, not objecting to a phrase or a sentiment because it came from Shakespeare or Scott, Dr. Johnson or Robert Burns.

Dr. Richard Glover of Bristol writes, "To listen to his talk on books, one would think that he had done nothing but read in a library all his life, and to mark publications, would fancy that he had done nothing but write."

This is imprressive, to say the least, but it appears that Spurgeon was almost super-human. What does that average reader take away from this? Does this encourage us to dig in and read more, or does it frighten us a bit because we can not possibly live up to these kinds of Olympian literary fetes? This is, however, a good motivational story that shows the fruit of sacrifice and hours spent in dedication to reading.

Hopefully, this encourages us to Puritan-like self-examination (something Spurgeon would certainly encourage for anyone). Hopefully, as well, instead of discouragement, we find a role model and someone to emulate.

"If it is asked what Mr. Spurgeon himself read, the answer is that he read everything...."

Several universities gave him honorary degrees, but he put them aside, and he did not encourage his students to seek academic honors."

Simply stated, Spurgeon read everything.

"No matter what his rank or position may be, the lover of books is the richest and the happiest of the children of men."

John Alfred Langford

Theodore Roosevelt
President of the United States
1901-1908

***Read a Book a Day for All of His Adult
Life
Two or Three Books During Slow Nights
in the White House
150,000 Letters in His Public Career***

Biographical Sketch

Born:

October 27, 1858

Early Reading Influence:
Aunt Anna Bulloch

Education:
Harvard BA

Leadership:
Governor of New York 1898
Vice President of U.S.-1900
President of U.S. -1901 (served 2 terms)
Roosevelt accomplished many other things
and wrote 37 books in his lifetime.

Died:

January 6, 1919

Roosevelt Read
Twenty Thousand Books

Teddy Roosevelt was born in 1858. He loved the outdoors during his youth—everything to do with the outdoors. An early story reveals this (taken from Judson's *Theodore Roosevelt, Fighting Patriot*):
His mother exclaimed,
> 'Theodore, look at this room...and smell it! See that piece of skin on your dresser and that bird wing. That snake—it's been dead weeks. How you ever found a snake in the city I do not know...all these things must be thrown out!'

Teddy answered,
> 'Mother! How can you say that! Think of the loss to science. These specimens are for the Roosevelt Museum. They are for the education of generations yet unborn' (Judson, p. 16).

Young Roosevelt became interested in books by looking at the pictures from missionary David Livingstone's *Missionary Travels and Researches in Southern Africa*. Morris comments, "Teddy opened it, and found within a world he could happily inhabit the rest of his days." Even though he understood the pictures, he stayed in Livingstone's book for weeks.

Theodore Roosevelt, eventually, read twenty thousand books. That breaks down to a book a day from the age of eight (*Theodore Rex*, Morris, p. 11).

Several biographers point out that the earliest reading Roosevelt did for himself was the **Layman's Look at Mammals** written by Mayne Reid. Morris states, "He pored endlessly over these in the library, curled up in a tiny chair which became his favorite article of furniture." Roosevelt writes in his autobiography, "When my father found how deeply interested I was in this not very accurate volume, he gave me a little book by J.G. Wook, the English writer of popular books on natural history, and then a larger one of his called, **Homes Without Hands**" (p. 17).

Like Harry Truman, Teddy Roosevelt had very poor eyesight. Also like Truman, Teddy's poor eyesight stopped him from nothing. He read all the time, even obsessively, as a lad. Because of his poor health, Roosevelt did not go to school with the other kids his age. Anna Bulloch, his aunt, tutored him. Anna taught him for an hour each morning. She allowed young Teddy to read from the downstairs library—anything he wished to read. His voracious reading gave him an unusual vocabulary for a boy his age. Roosevelt commended his father, later, for not trying to overly direct his reading as a young boy (similar to the childhood experience of C.S. Lewis). Roosevelt's father simply encouraged what was good in young Teddy. Whitelaw writes,

> Teddy's days were never long enough to satisfy him. Besides working out, he wanted to read more and to learn more. One of his friends called him 'the most studious little brute I ever knew in my life.' Private tutors taught him English, French, German, Latin and taxidermy, the art of preparing, stuffing and mounting the skins of dead animals (p. 23).

At the age of fourteen he was sent off to the country in order to strengthen himself against his persistent youth-related asthma. His literary interests persisted through this period. He met with his cousins on Sunday afternoons to read original stories and poems. He studied six to eight hours daily, five days a week, for the Harvard entrance examination's math, Latin and Greek sections. He took his eight-part Harvard University entrance examination in July of 1875, which he passed with relative ease.

Seventeen-year-old Teddy Roosevelt entered Harvard University in the fall of 1876, and graduated Magna Cum Laude in 1880. He ranked twenty-first in a class of 177. During his time there, Teddy developed a reputation in several different respects. His own opinion of Harvard, however, was rather tainted. He writes in his autobiography, "In the fall of 1876, I entered Harvard, graduating in 1880. I thoroughly enjoyed Harvard, and I am sure it did me good, but only in the general effect, for there was very little in my actual studies which helped me in after life" (p. 22). As well, Roosevelt mentioned only one Harvard professor in his autobiography.

Whitelaw mentions,

Everyone knew that Theodore loved to talk. Because he read so much, he could discuss many different subjects—boxing, bird-watching, Abraham Lincoln, the Dead Sea—almost anything at all. 'Reading with me is a disease,' he said. He later explained how he remembered most of what he read. 'As I talked, the pages of the book came before my eyes' (p. 30).

Roosevelt knew the intellectual and academic "bright lights" of his day, but he was the most well-read of all of them. Marconi, Italian inventor of the radio, said, "That man actually cited book after book that I've never heard of, much less read. He's going to keep me busy for some time just following his Italian reading." Science fiction writer H.G. Wells writes, "His reading is amazing" (*Shelf Life*, George and Karen Grant, p. 133).

Roosevelt, at Harvard, managed to get through prodigious quantities of work (Morris, p. 89). This required diligent effort, which Roosevelt invested willingly.

When he was laid up with the measles in February of 1877, he canceled his Easter vacation to make up for lost time. He secluded himself on the farm of a friend and read "the first book of Horace, the sixth book of Homer, and the Apology of Socrates" in five days (p. 89).

Being a "B" man did not keep Roosevelt from telling his classmates and his professors what he thought on relevant topics. One contemporary stated, "He leaps to his feet again at a lecture, challenges the speaker's statements, then complains that the presentation is unclear" (Morris, p. 84). Another said, "Again and again he leaps to his feet at lectures, until a professor shouts angrily, 'See here, Roosevelt, let me talk. *I'm* running this course'" (Ibid.). Roosevelt worked hard in order to be so involved. He rose early and worked six to eight hours before breakfast. This left his afternoons and evenings open for romance (Morris, p. 114).

Wagenknecht writes, "He declined to do an honors thesis, preferring instead to begin work on his first book, ***The Naval War of 1812***." Roosevelt stated, later, that much of his ethic was taught him either from his reading at Harvard or his personal reading (Autobiography, p. 25). He also read his Bible constantly which greatly influenced his thought and writing. He actually included more than forty-two hundred references to Scripture in his published works.

Roosevelt continued to love the outdoors and reading, as well, during his post-Harvard days. He enjoyed a rather illustrious military career. He writes much about his literary bent. His biographers emphasize his Gulliver-like reading habits. If Jimmy Carter was a reading "Goliath," Teddy Roosevelt was a literary "Gulliver" with an appetite for reading as big as the world itself.

His biographers use the following words to describe his reading appetite: rapid and omnivorous; wide; remarkable; indefatigable; abundant; unabated; a disease; passion; amazing; absorption; incredible speed; better than many 'well-read' men do nowadays; savant; bookish; richness of...knowledge; omnivorous and insatiable.

Roosevelt's biographers mention the following works or authors read by the President: Poe; Lady Baltimore; David Graham Philips; Sarah Jewett; Mary Freeman; Octave Thanet; Zola; Rabelais; Boccaccio; Shakespeare; Bayard Veiller; Holmes; Thueydides; Carlyle; Froissard; Macaulay; Homer; Dante; Spenser; Milton; Shelley; Emerson; Longfellow; Tennyson; Keates; Harte; Bacon; Lowell; Euripides; Marlowe; Dickens; Thackeray; Cooper; Scott; Darwin; Goethe; Huxley; Aquinas; Bryan; Wells; Hadley; Travelyan; Connoly; Michelis; Lecky; Tolstoy; Matthew Arnold; Gibbon; Polybius; Tacitus; Livy; Aristotle; Plutarch; Herodotus; Lucretius; Vergil; Juvenal; Josephus; Sophocles; Marcus Aurelius; Chaucer; Dryden; Browning; Kipling; Masefield; Bunyan; Bacon; Pepys; Johnson; Chesterfield; Huxley; Spencer; Harrison; Lang; Chesterton; Fronde; Freeman; Dumas; Irving; Hawthorne; Cooper; Marvel; Burroughs; Cable; Craddock; Macon; Joel Chandler Harris; Sherwood Bonner; Blake; Whittier; Montaigne; Whitman; Twain; William Dean Howells; Henry James; Stephen Crane; Ambrose Bierece; Frank Stockton; Richard Davis; Frank Norris; John Fox Jr.; Owen Wiste; William Allen White; Churchill; Robert Grant; Branch Cabell; Elise Singmaster; Stanley Waterloo; Kathleen Norris; Prescott; Motley; Parkman; Brooks Adams; Arsene Lupin; Alfred Henry Lewis; Emerson Hough; Villon Ronsard; Mistral Korner; Topelius; Sylva; Fogazzaro; Henry Bordeaus; Tenger; Balzac; Sienkiewicz; Charles Wagner; Foulkes; Dickinson; Trollope; DeQuincey; Tacitus; Samuel Dill; Jacobs; Scott;— the list could go on and on.

The biographers actually chronicle many more authors and books than these but no doubt, I have illustrated the point successfully.

Roosevelt read quantities of literature that could only be labeled as "phenomenal." But, you may ask, did he actually remember what he read?

Biographer Edmund Morris writes:

Theodore Roosevelt's memory can, in the opinion of the historian George Otto Trvelyan, be compared with the legendary mechanism of Thomas Babington Macaulay. Authors are embarrassed, ruing Presidential audiences, to hear long quotes from their work, which they themselves have forgotten. Congressmen know that it is useless to contest him on facts. Roosevelt recited 'almost verbatim, a long piece of Hungarian historical literature'...Roosevelt says he has neither seen nor thought of the document in twenty years.

He was asked to explain a similar performance before a Chinese delegation. Roosevelt explained that the book pages would simply come before his eyes (even if it was a book he had read some time before). It would seem as if these pages swam before his eyes. When he would see someone face-to-face, he would put his hands over his eyes to visualize where he had seem that person before.

Is it possible that continued and steady reading can increase ones memory retention? Wagenknecht insists that Roosevelt did not have "photographic memory" because of the number of misspellings he found in Roosevelt's work (Wagenknecht, p. 74). Somehow, Roosevelt remembered almost miraculous amounts of material (verbatim) and the method may never be adequately known, except to take Roosevelt at his word.

Roosevelt's obvious mnemonic genius matched his indefatigable effort and humility. Roosevelt constantly learned and read wherever he went. He stated, "Books are the greatest of companions" (Wagenknecht, p. 44).

William Howard Taft states, "He always carried a book with him to the Executive office and although there were but few intervals during the business hours, he made the most of them in his reading." Roosevelt even kept a book on the table near the front door to read while waiting for Mrs. Roosevelt when they were going somewhere together. As well, Roosevelt read French books all the way from San Antonio to Tampa on his way from the Spanish American War.

Biographers underscore Roosevelt's ability to concentrate completely as a key to his gargantuan reading accomplishment: "Even in childhood Roosevelt had the fortunate capacity of complete absorption in his reading. His cousin, Emlen Roosevelt, says that the only way to get his attention when he was reading was to strike him on the back" (Ibid. p. 45). This ability to concentrate continued right through to his days in the White House. Wagenknecht writes,

> The most interesting thing, however, is the conditions under which Roosevelt managed to do some of his classical reading. He read both Thucydides and Josephus during the 1900 convention and the Anabasis on a western trip in 1903. Dean Lewis found him reading Herodotus during the 1912 convention while the band was playing and the crowd outside shouting, 'We want Teddy!' During his South American trip, however, the classics would seem to have failed T.B. He took Marcus Aurelius and Sophocles with him, 'but when he tried to read them during the descent of the Rio da Duvida,' says Kermit, 'they only served to fill him with indignation at their futility. Some translations

of Greek plays…met with but little better success'
(Ibid. p. 50).

Roosevelt could read under impossible conditions and
the worst possible reading circumstances. Roosevelt's
assistant, Lawrence Abbott, writes
"I searched the train for him and finally
discovered him in one of the white enameled lavatories
with its door half open where, standing under an
electric light, he was busily engaged in reading, while
he braced himself in the angle of the two walls against
the swaying motion of the train, oblivious to time and
surrounding. The book in which he was absorbed
was Leeky's *History of Rationalism in Europe*.
He had chosen this peculiar reading room both
because the white enamel reflected a brilliant light and
he was pretty sure of uninterrupted quiet…he
borrowed from prisoners (whom he had helped
capture in Dakota) on his way home *The History of
the James Brothers*!
Sometimes in Africa, he read from his famous
'Pigskin Library' 'resting under a tree at noon, perhaps
beside the carcass of a beast he had killed, or else
while waiting for camp to be pitched; and in either
case it might be impossible to get water for washing.
In consequence, the books were stained with blood,
sweat, gun-oil, dust, and ashes; ordinary bindings
either vanished or became loathsome, whereas pigskin
merely grew to look as a well-used saddle looks.'
Sometimes when he got in from the field, he wrote his
sister. He could not settle down to write his hunting
articles until he had first spent an hour or two reading.
But even this was nothing compared to his
achievements in South America, where Kermit would
find him propped against a tree reading Gibbon or

The Oxford Book of French Verse when he was too sick to hold himself up without help (Ibid. p. 47).

Other historians record instances of Roosevelt's constant reading, right through sickness and grief over friends and loved ones. O.K. Davis says,

> [Roosevelt] always had a great deal of reading matter with him, which he supplemented along the way by buying all the new magazines. The character of the magazine did not seem to make any difference to him...I have seen him again and again read a magazine from cover to cover, everything in it, special articles, poetry, stories and all. And as he read it he would tear out the finished page and throw it to the floor, just as he did the pages of manuscript when delivering a speech (Ibid. p. 69).

Roosevelt never passed up the chance to dip into literature (Morris p. 139). Morris writes,

> We fairly stand amazed, and cannot but look upon this man as a marvel...Apparently this indefatigable student never sinks back in his chair to rest his brain and his body. The book is always at hand and is snatched up to fill any interval which others give to reposeful relaxation...His college classmates tell us that, while visiting the rooms of his fellow students, he would at any pause in the tide of talk be apt to pick up a book and quickly become so absorbed in its contents as to forget all around him. Then, suddenly becoming aware of his lack of politeness, he would hurry away with guilty haste from the room and the raillery of his companions. This was always his habit— to bury himself in his book, and become so lost in it as to forget all around him. He fairly lived in the book,

and had a remarkable faculty of getting out of it all of the value it contained (Morris, p. 138,139).

In some ways, Thomas Jefferson read similarly as a student—fifteen hours a day. "Jefferson could not live without his books" (See *Jefferson*, Konecky & Konecky Publishers, Saul Padover, p. 14, 128).

Concerning people publishing favorite book lists, Roosevelt had neither time nor sympathy for such practices but said,

> It is all right for a man to amuse himself by composing a list of a hundred very good books; and if he is to go off for a year or so where he cannot get many books, it is an excellent thing to choose a five-foot library of particular books which in that particular year and on that particular trip he would like to read (autobiography p. 334).

Roosevelt kept it up, diligently, right into and through the White House. This is as mind-boggling as the reading itself. He even wrote a book review on a book about pheasants on the day he died.

He wrote massive amounts of personal letters (150,000 personal letters in his career). Morris writes about a record which Roosevelt set in January of 1907. Roosevelt shook 8,150 hands. This feat would remain unbroken for seventy-two years.

Roosevelt's reading habits give us the x-ray diagnosis on his diligence:

> As quietness settles down over the Presidential apartments, Roosevelt and his wife will sit by the fire in the Prince of Wales Room and read to each other. At about ten o'clock the First Lady will rise and kiss her husband good night. He will continue to read in the light of a student lamp, peering

through his one good eye (the other is blind) at the book held inches from his nose, flicking over the page at a rate of two or three a minute.

This is the time of the day he loves best.

'Reading with me is a disease.' He succumbs to it so totally—on the heaving deck of the Presidential yacht in the middle of a cyclone, between whistle-stops on a campaign trip, even while waiting for his carriage at the front door—that nothing short of a thump on the back will regain his attention. Asked to summarize the book he has been leafing through with such apparent haste, he will do so in minute detail, often quoting the actual text (Morris, p. 28).

Roosevelt would read a book a day, even if he was busy. Someone could hand him a book in the evening and hear a full report on it over breakfast the next morning. This was done even when he had been entertaining guests the night before!

On the evenings when he had nothing to do, he would read two or three books in their entirety.

This Harvard "B" man devoured a book a night in the White House on busy nights, and on slow nights the Harvard "B" man consumed two or three books and wrote a book review on the day of his death. After retiring from the White House, Thomas Jefferson continued reading Greek diligently into his twilight years (Padover, p. 412).

Unlike Jefferson, who found little time to read as President, we leave President Theodore Roosevelt with his usual open book on his desk in the oval office.

"Read at every wait; read at all hours; read within leisure; read about in times of labor; read as one goes in; read as one goes out. The task of the educated mind is simply put: read to lead."

Cicero (Roman Statesman, Orator, Writer)
106-43 B.C.

What Can We Learn From These Leaders?

We learn several lessons from these seven men who were born in different centuries on different continents.

First, they all started early in life. Lewis, Carson, and Nader read voraciously as pre-teenagers. Spurgeon and all of the others began, in earnest, somewhere in their early years. Spurgeon read Milton as a lad; he re-read Milton a hundred times throughout the rest of his life.

Second, elders influenced them to read while they were young. There seemed to have been no substitute for others around them, leading them by example as kids. The Mothers of Truman, Carter, Carson and (to a lesser extent) Lewis led them by reading example.

Third, formal education meant different things to these men. Truman scoffed at formal education and specifically textbooks used in schools. He went to work and not to college after high school. Spurgeon was rejected from entering college. Roosevelt was a "B" man at Harvard and constantly argued publicly with his professors. Nader was brilliant at Princeton as an undergraduate student and rebellious at Harvard Law School. Carson overachieved at Johns Hopkins in an unorthodox fashion—he rarely went to class. Carter and Lewis buried everybody everywhere they went to school.

Fourth, all of these men placed high value on reading. They did not simply read; they valued books. Truman carried books to his clothing shop workplace. Spurgeon had a library of over ten thousand books. Roosevelt said reading was "a disease" with him (his own words). Ralph Nader reads consumer letters as a semi-religious experience (according to some of his co-workers). Lewis felt that going to a bookshop was one of his greatest temptations because he would always want to buy something. Like John Ruskin, he felt that if a book was worth reading it was worth reading over and over—thus worth buying. Carter always asked for books on his birthday. Carson states over and over his belief in books.

Fifth, these men read broadly diverse books. Roosevelt read his Bible often as well as the Greeks. Carter read nuclear physics and the Bible in Spanish. Carson reads medical journals and fiction. Truman read a library. Spurgeon read Shakespeare and the Puritans. Nader reads no fiction. Lewis was well read at the age of eight.

Sixth, and probably the most important lesson from all of these men is their life-long habit of diligent pereseverant reading. They truly obey Cicero's dictum: "Read at evey wait, read at all hours, read within leisure; read about in times of labor; read as one goes in; read as one goes out. The task of the educated mind is simply put: read to lead." Carter reads at the breakfast table, Roosevelt read while waiting for his wife at the front door of the White House, Spurgeon's read a book a day throughout his life, Truman's daughter stated that she could not remember ever seeing him without a book in his hands. All of this points to life-long diligent reading; something all of us can learn from their lives.

Finally, we might ask, "What can we do to change our own reading habits?" Psychologists tell us that it takes three months to change a habit. I have a few ideas. First, carry a book wherever we go. I think of Roosevelt when I suggest this. Remember the old President deliberately leaving his book open on his desk in the White House. Edmund Morris, Roosevelt's biographer, tells us that Roosevelt retreated to this open book any time his visitors became boring.

A second idea would be to schedule fifteen to thirty minutes a day of new reading for the next quarter and stick to it with iron clad determination. I think setting goals is extremely important for reading success.

A third idea is to mingle with other readers. Talk with them about books. Start a reading group which meets weekly (only to read for an hour or two). I have close friends that have done this and found it to be very helpful in accomplishing reading goals.

A fourth idea, watch "Book TV" on C-Span television. I have learned a lot from some of the great minds of our time doing this passive activity.

A fifth and final idea, perhaps we should not start a second book until we have finished reading the first one. How many people do you know who say that they read about ten books at a time? If you ask them how many they finish, sometimes the number may be disappointing.

"Read at every wait; read at all hours; read within leisure; read about in times of labor; read as one goes in; read as one goes out. The task of the educated mind is simply put: read to lead."

Cicero

Bibliography

General Books:

Booknotes:America's Finest Authors on Reading, Writing, and the Power of Ideas, Brian Lamb, Crown Publishing, 1997.

A Passion for Books, Terry W. Glaspey, Harvest House Publishers, 1998.

Shelf Life, George Grant and Karen Grant, Cumberland House Publishing, 1999.

Unstoppable, Cynthia Kersey, Sourcebooks, 1998.

Jimmy Carter

Dasher:The Roots and Rising of Jimmy Carter, James Wooten, Summit Books, 1978.

Why Not the Best?, James Earl Carter, Bantam Books, 1976.

The Carpenter's Apprentice:The Spiritual Biography of Jimmy Carter, Dan Ariall, Harper-Collins/Zondervan, 1996.

Jimmy Carter, The Man and the Myth, Victor Lasky, Putnam Books, 1979.

Ralph Nader

Citizen Nader, Charles McCarry, Saturday Review Press, 1972.

Nader, The People's Lawyer, Robert Buckhorn, Prentice-Hall, 1972.

Charles Spurgeon

The Unforgettable Spurgeon, Eric Hayden, Emerald Books, 1997.

Spurgeon:Prince of Preachers, Lewis Drummond, Kregel Publishers, 1992.

131 Christians Everybody Should Know, Broadman and Holman Publishers, 2000.

C.S. Lewis

The C.S. Lewis Encyclopedia, Colin Duriez, Crosswy Books, 2000.

Jack:A Life of C.S. Lewis, George Sayer, Crossway Books, 1994.

Harry Truman

Plain Speaking: An Oral Biography of Harry S. Truman, Merle Miller, Berkley, 1974.

President from Missouri, Ralph G. Martin,

The Man from Missouri, Alfred Steinbereg, Putnam, 1962.

Mr. President, Hilman

Truman, David McCullough, Simon and Schuster, 1992.

Theodore Roosevelt
Theodore Roosevelt, Fighting Patriot, Clara Judsono, Follett Publishing, 1954.

The Rise of Theodore Roosevelt, Edmund Morris, Ballantine Books, 1986.

Theodore Roosevelt Takes Charge, Nancy Whitelaw and Abby Levine, Albert Whiteman & Co. 1992.

The Seven Worlds of Theodore Roosevelt, Edward Wagenknecht, Longmans, Green and Co., 1958.

Impressions of Theodore Roosevelt, Lawrence Abbott, Doubleday Page And Co., 1922.

Dr. Benjamin Carson
Gifted Hands:The Ben Carson Story, Dr. Ben Carson, Zondervan, 1990.

Think Big, Ben Carson, Morrow, 1993.

On the Web

www.ronsmithbooks.com